The
Stock
Market

—

the real world series

The
Stock
Market

Marc Rosenblum

Lerner Publications Company—Minneapolis, Minnesota

ACKNOWLEDGMENTS

The illustrations are reproduced through the courtesy of: pp. 8-9, 17, 22, 34, 36-37, 40, 47, 87, New York Stock Exchange; p. 11, General Telephone and Electronics Corporation; pp. 14, 15, Library of Congress; pp. 19, 23, Smithsonian Institution; pp. 25, 26, 44-45, American Stock Exchange; pp. 32, 41, 42, Paine, Webber, Jackson, and Curtis, News Photo Service; p. 49, Bankers Trust Company, Mario Marino, photographer; p. 55, National Archives, United States Office of War Information; p. 61, Savings Bond Division, United States Treasury Department; pp. 66, 67, 79, Independent Picture Service; p. 72, Merrill Lynch, Pierce, Fenner, and Smith, Inc.; p. 76, General Motors Corporation, Cadillac Motor Car Division; p. 84, Farmers and Mechanics Savings Bank of Minneapolis.

photo editor: Judith Murphy

The Library of Congress cataloged the
original printing of this title as follows:

Rosenblum, Marc.
    The stock market.   Minneapolis, Lerner Publications Co.
[1970]

    94 p. illus., ports. 23 cm. (The Real World Series)

    Traces the history of America's stock market, explains how it functions and is regulated, and analyzes its importance to the United States economy.

    1. Stock-exchange—U. S.—Juvenile literature. [1. Stock exchange] I. Title.

HG4553.R66	332.6′1	76-84418
ISBN 0-8225-0615-7		MARC
		AC

International Standard Book Number: 0-8225-0615-7
Library of Congress Catalog Card Number: 76-84418

Second Printing 1972

Contents

There is nothing like the ticker tape . . . nothing that promises, hour after hour, day after day, such sudden developments; nothing that disappoints so often or occasionally fulfills with such unbelievable, passionate magnificence.

WALTER KNOWLETON GUTMAN

Introduction

It is exactly 10 A.M. While we are standing on a balcony, overlooking a large room crowded with people, a buzzer sounds. A small cheer goes up from the throng, followed by the steady hum of activity. Men dash about, waving their arms. Others jot notes on small pads. A movie-type screen lights up, and a steady stream of numbers and letters flash across it. What is going on?

This scene, repeated every business day, is the start of trading on the New York Stock Exchange, or the Big Board, as it is called. Here, along with the

American Stock Exchange, regional exchanges, and over-the-counter trading, is the force behind America's industrial economy. The stock market is a complex mechanism which allows for the exchange of securities and provides a meeting place for buyers and sellers. Both corporate stocks (shares of ownership)

The trading floor of the New York Stock Exchange, the world's largest market for securities.

and bonds (long term debt) are traded in these markets. In related trading, bonds of the federal government and its agencies are also bought and sold.

Without this system of markets, the national economy of the United States could not operate as smoothly or as efficiently as it does. For business corporations, the stock market is a source of capital (money) to operate and expand their activities. For persons with money to invest, the stock market provides an opportunity to participate in business ventures. Neither party has to know the other, for they engage in the transaction through a prearranged system and set of understandings.

What the market does, then, is to bring together interested parties from all over the country through intermediaries (brokers and investment bankers) without the parties having to leave their homes. It is one of the most important institutions in America's economic system, and provides a functional means of channeling money into productive uses.

Corporate Capitalization

In the American industrial system, most important business firms are large corporations, worth many millions of dollars each. Unless a new or expanding company has access to capital resources, however, its chances of success are limited. These resources are obtained by selling stocks and bonds.

A new corporation selling shares, or one issuing bonds or additional shares, first sells them to an *underwriter*, or investment banker. (Many times the underwriting is done by a *syndicate*, or group of investment bankers.) In return, the corporation receives

General Telephone & Electronics Corporation (GT&E) has filed with the Securities and Exchange Commission a Registration Statement under the Securities Act of 1933 with respect to $150,000,000 in aggregate principal amount of its 5% Subordinated Convertible Debentures, Due 1992 (the New Debentures).

General Telephone

&

Electronics Corporation

CONTENTS

PROSPECTUS

Neither the delivery of this Prospectus nor any sales made hereunder shall under any circumstances create any implication that there has been no change in the affairs of GT&E since the date hereof. No dealer, salesman or any other person has been authorized to give any information or to make any representations other than those contained in this Prospectus and, if given or made, such information or representations must not be relied upon. This Prospectus does not constitute an offering by GT&E or the Underwriters in any state in which such offering may not be lawfully made.

Until January 29, 1968 all dealers effecting transactions in the registered securities, whether or not participating in this distribution, may be required to deliver a Prospectus. This is in addition to the obligation of dealers to deliver a Prospectus when acting as Underwriters and with respect to their unsold allotments or subscriptions.

A prospectus gives information concerning a company's past performance and growth potential. When a company issues new stock, this booklet is made available to prospective buyers.

the proceeds, or value of the stock, less underwriting charges for helping the corporation in the sale.

The underwriter resells the stock to brokers representing investors who are interested in owning shares of the offered company. A *prospectus*, or information booklet, is made available to prospective buyers at the initial *offering* — the first time the stock is put up for sale to the public. A prospectus is also published with offerings of any new securities of the corporation — either stocks or bonds. The company's past record, capitalization and growth potential are outlined in the prospectus.

The Growth of the Corporation

Trading of corporate securities in the United States is almost as old as the country itself, but the practice did not gain importance until the major growth of the corporation. This growth occurred only after the separate states passed general laws of incorporation. In 1812 New York passed the first statute, allowing anyone to apply for the incorporation of his business. By 1850 the other states had followed suit. Prior to that time, a corporate charter was granted to an applicant only by legislative action. This practice limited the number of applicants to those persons with political connections.

Another factor in corporate growth was the increase in the scale of business throughout America's economy. Business firms expanded in size and capacity to gain competitive advantage. In order to expand, however, they had to raise large sums for facilities and equipment. Individual business owners or even most partnership agreements could not raise the necessary capital by themselves.

The only form of business organization suited to large-scale capitalization was the corporation. Furthermore, corporate shareholders were not held liable for business losses beyond the value of their investment, while private businessmen did not have this protection.

In the decades following the Civil War, industry expanded rapidly. The settling of the West, the millions immigrating from Europe and the widespread use of electric power all contributed to economic growth. In this setting, trading in stocks and bonds thrived. As the nation grew, more issues were traded, but not all companies survived or were successful. Periodic depressions wiped out some investors, but others replaced them in financing the growth of industry. For the successful, profits were spectacular and fortunes were made.

America's past history is filled with clever but dishonest men who became millionaires by taking advantage of the government's lack of securities regulation during the late 1800s. Since then, both state and federal regulation of the securities business has created a more honest and stable environment for investors. Risks, of course, are always present. The business world remains full of uncertainties and this is translated into fluctuating stock prices. Nevertheless, more Americans than ever before now own publicly traded securities.

Cornelius Vanderbilt (left) and John Pierpont Morgan (above) amassed great fortunes in the industrial expansion of the late nineteenth century. They were involved in corporate growth at a time when there was no federal regulation of securities.

1

The History of Securities
Trading in the United States

The New York Stock Exchange

The name "Wall Street" has come to represent not only the investment community in New York, but the financial image of the United States all over the world. "The Street," as it is known, is the center of the New York financial district which contains the two major stock exchanges — the New York and the American — as well as brokerage houses, banking firms, commodity trading, and the main offices of many large

An outside view of the New York Stock Exchange, Wall Street, New York City.

corporations. Wall Street's association with securities trading dates back to post-Revolutionary War days.

Although there is no wall on Wall Street now, there was one once, erected under the direction of Peter Stuyvesant in 1653. New York was then still a Dutch settlement called New Amsterdam, and Stuyvesant was its governor. The wall was needed to keep the colony's animals from straying into the wilderness, and to protect the settlement from Indian attack.

Philadelphia, rather than New York, was considered the young country's banking center when the seat of the national government was shifted there from New York in 1790. There was a small stock exchange in Philadelphia, while trading in New York remained more informal. Stockbrokers at that time also had other businesses, which they regarded as more important than selling a small number of stocks and bonds.

In good weather, New York brokers met out on Wall Street under an old buttonwood tree. Otherwise they congregated in coffeehouses and restaurants — particularly the Tontine Coffee House. (When trading wasn't going on, meals were served.) On May 17, 1792, 24 of these brokers signed an agreement granting preference to one another in the trading of stocks

The founding of the New York Stock Exchange. In 1792, 21 individuals and three partnerships signed an agreement to establish a private market for securities.

and stating that the commission they charged would not be less than one-fourth of one percent of the value of the transaction. This agreement is considered to be the founding of the New York Stock Exchange, the name the group took much later, in 1863.

Prior to the War of 1812, America was primarily agricultural and most manufactured goods were imported from Europe. Since little manufacturing was taking place, the majority of stocks traded were those of banks or insurance companies.

Most businesses of this early period were owned individually or in partnership. Profits were reinvested into the firm to pay for expansion. Outside capital was generally unnecessary, as the size and scope of most firms was small. To those early capitalists, it did not seem sensible to sell shares in their business to outsiders when they could personally provide the necessary funds. It was not until industry outgrew this infant stage and incorporations increased that the stock market became a vital part of America's economy.

In 1817, about 20 brokers and brokerage houses formally organized into the New York Stock and Exchange Board. The brokers used the rules of the Philadelphia exchange as the model for their constitution. They also moved their trading indoors — to the second story of a house at 40 Wall Street, which they soon outgrew as trading in securities became increasingly popular.

The construction of canals during the 1820s and of railroads after 1830 was of great importance to the growth of the stock market. Shareholders were sought to provide the vast sums required to clear the land, put down tracks, and buy locomotives. Railroad stocks were widely traded, and were even responsible for the first large-scale investment by European bankers in America. The money flowing in from abroad helped open transportation routes to the West faster than would otherwise have been possible.

The invention of the telegraph in 1844 made nationwide communication with Wall Street possible. Following the Civil War, large-scale economic expansion became common. Financing industry and commerce brought wealth and fame to investment bankers who controlled many large firms. Noted for their ruthless (and sometimes dishonest) tactics, men like Cornelius Vanderbilt, Jay Gould, James Fisk, Daniel Drew, Edward Harriman, and J. P. Morgan — all of whom made fortunes on railroads — were both admired and feared. To friends they were "captains of industry." Many others called them "robber barons."

In 1867 the stock ticker was invented by E. A. Calahan. This machine, which printed quotations of prices and bids on paper tape, was installed in brokers' offices to replace messengers and to provide trading information quickly. By 1869 the exchange had become the New York Stock Exchange, with 1,060 members, and had moved into a building close to the site of its present home, the corner of Wall and Broad Streets.

The first stock ticker, 1867. This ticker was used until 1883 when it was replaced by a domed apparatus developed by Thomas Edison. Edison's stock ticker could print 285 characters a minute.

At the present time, the New York Stock Exchange has 1,366 memberships, or *seats*, most of which are held by partners in member firms and officers of member corporations. Other seats are held by individuals. These seats are valuable, since the number is limited to 1,366 and the members who hold them are the only ones permitted to trade directly on the exchange. Non-members must give their orders to a member firm and pay commissions on each transaction.

In the mid-nineteenth century, a seat on the New York Stock Exchange represented a chair in a large rented hall. Each member broker owned the chair on which he sat. Only member brokers were allowed in the room. A call system of trading was used whereby, after a stock was named, individuals could shout bids from their seats.

A prospective member of the exchange must first arrange to buy a seat from a member who is willing to sell and then his membership must be approved by exchange officials. The price of New York Stock Exchange seats fluctuates. They have sold for as little as $17,000 in 1942 and as much as $625,000 in 1929. Brokerage houses are not limited in the number of seats they may own. Some of the largest firms own a dozen or more seats.

Other Exchanges

As other cities became regional centers of industry, local stock exchanges opened up. Over the years some exchanges prospered, some failed, and others merged into larger organizations.

The second largest securities market in the United States is also in New York. It is called the American Stock Exchange. Until 1953 it was known as the Curb Exchange, because prior to 1921 it had operated on the sidewalks of Broad Street, just blocks from the New York Exchange. Wall Streeters, in fact, still refer to this exchange as "the Curb."

In general, the companies and corporations listed on the American Stock Exchange are smaller and often younger companies than those listed on the Big Board. The American Stock Exchange, however, is the largest market for foreign securities in the United States.

Unusually patterned and colored hats identified each broker of the Curb Exchange. Here, a curb broker signals to his clerk in an adjoining building. The system of hand signals employed on the street is still used by the American Stock Exchange.

The Midwest Exchange in Chicago and the Pacific Coast Exchange in both Los Angeles and San Francisco are next most important in annual volume of shares and money value traded. Smaller regional exchanges are located in Philadelphia, Detroit, Boston, Cincinnati, Pittsburgh, Spokane, Salt Lake City, Colorado Springs, Richmond, Va., and Honolulu, Hawaii.

One new exchange, the National, began in New York in 1962. Still small, its volume has jumped in recent years. By the end of 1971, more than 125 stocks were listed on the National Exchange.

Over-the-Counter Markets

Many stocks and bonds are not traded on exchanges, but are available to investors in the *over-the-counter market* (OTC) — a network of brokers connected by telephone, teletype, and computers. About 15,000 stocks trade actively, and twice that number inactively, in this market. Most bank and insurance stocks, and almost all government bonds, are traded OTC. About 80 percent of all bonds are unlisted. Smaller industrial firms, and some large ones that do not want to be listed on an exchange, also trade in this market. All new corporations begin trading over-the-counter, although some apply for listing on an exchange as soon as certain requirements are met.

The Third Market

Over the last few years a new form of trading has developed called the *third market*. (The first market is the exchange listing and the second OTC.) In the third market, listed stocks are sold over-the-counter by independent brokers. They compete with the exchanges, which were the exclusive source of listed stocks until this practice began. Now, a small but growing share of the market in listed stocks is handled by *third market* traders.

Listing on Exchanges

To be listed on the New York Stock Exchange, a company's securities should have a market value of at least $12 million. The firm must have net earnings after taxes of $1.2 million; not less than one million common shares outstanding (publicly issued and sold), of which at least 700,000 must be publicly held; and a minimum of 2,000 stockholders, of which at least 1,700 must own 100 shares apiece. There are other conditions, but the above are the most important ones.

Stocks of the largest and most widely held American corporations may be listed on both the New York and regional exchanges. IBM (International Business Machines Corporations), for example, is traded on the New York Exchange and also on the Midwest, Pacific Coast, and five other regional exchanges. Stocks may not, however, be listed on both the New York and American exchanges.

2

The Trading Process

Over-the-Counter Trading

Over-the-counter transactions are different from exchange trading. OTC trading is done through negotiation — by phone or wire — between brokers representing buyers or sellers on one hand, and professional dealers who *make a market* in the stock. "Making a market" means that dealers specialize in certain securities and stand ready to buy or sell them. The dealers indicate their *bid price* (what they will pay for a stock) and an *offer* (how much they will charge to sell it). The difference, or spread, is their profit.

Since 1971, a sophisticated computer system has allowed dealers to list their bid and offer electronically. Every brokerage house is linked to this computer, and the quotations on each stock appear on a special TV screen. Code symbols allow quotes on different issues to be shown, just like changing the channel on a home set.

The whole computer system is called National Association of Securities Dealers Automated Quotes, or NASDAQ (Nas-dack).

Let us follow a stock transaction through the over-the-counter market. For example, Ed Jones wants to buy 100 shares of Square Circle Company. He calls his broker and the conversation may sound like this:

Jones: "What is the market on Square Circle? I'm interested in buying 100 shares at 21 ($21 a share) or better."

Broker: "Hold on, I'll check." He quickly presses the stock's code symbol, the letters S-Q-C, on a smaller electronic machine. The price 21 ($21.00 a share) shows up. He now tells the client: "Mr. Jones, we should be able to get it for you. I'm placing the order."

The broker then places an order with his firm's trading department. A trader in the trading department, seated before his special screen, dials for the quotes on S-Q-C. Each dealer's bid and offer is shown. Usually, there is a slight difference between dealers, although not usually more than a quarter point for the same stock at the same time. In this particular case, two dealers are quoting 21. One shows 21 ($21.125), and the other shows 20 ($20.75).

Because the median price was 21 (the middle range of the two above offers), that figure was shown on the smaller quotation machine on the broker's desk. The trader, connected by phone to all the dealers making the market in that stock, calls the one offering the stock at 20¾ and makes the purchase. He then notifies the broker who in turn phones his client.

Broker: "Mr. Jones, we got it for you at 20¾."

Jones: "Thanks, I'll send you a check."

Had the market for Square Circle been higher than

Ed Jones's offer, he would not have gotten the stock unless he raised his bid. As an alternative, however, Mr. Jones could have left an open order with his broker to buy the stock if it dropped to a price of 21 or less.

In effect, over-the-counter dealers make a wholesale market, buying from and selling to brokerage firms representing clients. Most brokerage houses dealing with the public do not also trade over-the-counter stocks as a dealer (for their own account), although several of the largest do. An investor must "pay the spread" (sell on the dealer's bid, buy on his offer) in addition to paying the broker's commission similar to that on listed stocks. That is the disadvantage in owning over-the-counter securities.

Over-the-counter dealers belong to an association called the National Association of Securities Dealers, or NASD. Members who have registered with the Securities and Exchange Commission (SEC) are permitted to use the National Daily Quotation Service to advertise bid or offer prices. This service publishes the *pink sheets* — daily printed reports listing the prices at which OTC dealers throughout the country will buy or sell various securities, and the computer symbol for each security. The pink sheets, distributed to subscribing dealers each morning, also give the closing bid and offer for each security from the previous day. During each day price changes are made by the participating dealers depending on market conditions. Brokers whose clients want to trade a particular stock can see which dealers are prepared to negotiate a transaction with them.

Trading on the New York Stock Exchange

While over-the-counter markets are made in individual, negotiated transactions, stock exchanges operate as a continuous, hectic auction. The New York Stock Exchange floor is a huge room almost two-thirds the size of a football field. Activity centers around a series of horseshoe-shaped booths, called *posts*, where particular stocks are traded. There are 18 of these posts on the trading floor — each one listing about 75 stocks. Brokers know the location of the posts and frequently dash from one end of the floor to the other on successive trades.

Several types of brokers engage in trading on the floor of the exchange. Most brokers represent member firms that deal with the public, and they carry out orders from their firm's clients. They are called *floor brokers*, or *commission brokers*, since customers of the firm pay brokerage fees to have their orders filled.

Other brokers are called *specialists*. There are about 350 specialists who are exchange members, each handling several stocks. The specialist is important because he acts both as broker and dealer. In his capacity as a dealer, the specialist will buy or sell stocks from his own account to help maintain an *orderly market*, one in which prices do not fluctuate too widely or erratically, in his stock. As a broker, the specialist accepts orders in his special stocks from other brokers.

33

Brokers meet at a post on the New York Stock Exchange. Each post lists about 75 stocks.

He keeps these orders in his book (a black, loose-leaf notebook) until he can execute them at the prices the broker asks for. This releases the broker from waiting at the specialist's post until a trader appears. When the specialist fills the order, he will notify the broker.

At a post where a stock is popular and actively traded, several commission brokers will have orders to fill and will try to outbid each other for the best price. All bidding must be done in a loud voice so that interested parties may join in. Brokers wanting to buy the stock try to pay as little as possible, while sellers hope to receive a higher amount. Price fluctuations usually depend on whether more buyers or sellers are present, just like any other economic transaction. Sometimes two buyers call out the same price for the same amount of stock at the same time. When this happens, the competing brokers match coins, with the winner taking the stock.

Let's imagine that we are following Hank Green, floor broker for a large firm, at his work on the trading floor of the New York Stock Exchange. Hank's clerk, stationed at one of the booths around the floor, has just paged him by pressing a button that makes Hank's number flash on a large annunciator board. (Such boards are necessary because of the noise on the trading floor.) The clerk has received an order by teletype from the order room of Hank's firm, a few blocks away from the exchange. The order is to sell 100 shares of Slow-Leak Tire Corporation at $37 a share.

Brokers match coins to decide a stock transaction on the New York Stock Exchange.

Hank walks quickly to his clerk's booth, takes the order, and heads for the post where Slow-Leak Tire stock is being traded. He approaches the "crowd," or the group of brokers trading at that post. Hank asks: "How's Tire?" The specialist replies, "37 to one-quarter." This means that someone has offered to buy Slow-Leak Tire stock at $37 per share, but none is presently for sale below $37.25. Looking at the price indicator at the post, Hank sees that the last trade was at 37.

Hank knows that he can probably get 37, but hopes to get more for his firm's client. Another broker rushes up and shouts, "An eighth for 100." He is bidding 37⅛. Hank quickly points to the man and replies, "Sold." The transaction has been completed at 37⅛, or $3,712.50 for 100 shares. The two brokers each make a note of the transaction, while the exchange clerk at the post changes the indicator for Slow-Leak Tire to 37⅛. Then the two brokers dash off in opposite directions to inform their respective firms of the trade.

Most stocks trade in units of 100 shares, or a *round lot*. For the many small investors who cannot afford a round lot, there are brokers who provide a special service. They are called *odd-lot dealers*, and buy or sell *odd lots* (any number of shares less than the normal unit of trading). Odd-lot dealers buy for and sell from their own accounts. They do not deal with the public, but with other brokers. Investors pay an additional fee — besides commissions — which goes to these dealers for their service. Odd-lot transactions are made at the same price last traded on the floor for a round lot, with an extra 12½ cents a share on stock selling below $55, and 25 cents a share on stocks above $55, going to the odd-lot dealer. There are several odd-lot dealers at each trading post.

In addition, there are independent brokers, known as *registered traders*, who transact business for their own accounts. These brokers hold individual memberships in the exchange.

Commission brokers, specialists, odd-lot dealers, and registered traders are not the only men on the exchange floor. The so-called *two-dollar brokers* are independent registered brokers who prefer to handle transactions for other brokers (when they are busy) rather than trade for their own account. The name "two-dollar broker" originated when that was the fee paid for every 100-share order such brokers executed. Now this fee has changed, but the name "two-dollar broker" is still used.

There are also exchange employees on the trading floor. Clerks are located at each post to note price changes as trading proceeds. When a broker completes a transaction, or the specialist executes a trade, they hand the clerk a note with the price at which the

The "900," a modern stock ticker, can print up to 900 characters a minute.

transaction took place. The clerk, or floor reporter, transfers this information into coded boxes on a pre-printed card, which he inserts into a new device called an optical card-scanner. The scanner electronically feeds this transaction data into a computer which, in turn, "drives" the ticker tape.

As soon as possible, often within one minute of the trade, the transaction is printed on the ticker. Resembling an elongated movie screen, this device is visible from the trading floor and carries a steady flow of symbols and numbers representing transactions. Stock tickers are also installed in brokerage firms dealing with customers all over the country.

The ticker resembles a movie screen. Seen from the Exchange floor and in brokerage firms, it gives information regarding immediate transactions.

41

A brokerage office in New York City. Under the ticker is a board that electronically summarizes the activity of each listed stock.

Trading information is available to anyone interested enough to visit or telephone a broker's office. Electronic stock-quotation devices in brokerage firms also summarize activity in each listed stock, providing its opening, high, low, and last price, and the total volume traded that day.

In addition to the clerks stationed at the posts, there are clerks employed by the various brokers to process their paperwork and to notify their firms (in the case of commission brokers) of all transactions.

There are also floor officials appointed by the exchange's Board of Governors to oversee all trading. There are 33 governors: 29 of these are members or allied members elected by the membership; the three others, plus a president, are elected by the Board and have no connection with the securities business because they must represent the public viewpoint. The governors serve three-year terms and their function is to prevent dishonest dealings, to enforce exchange rules and policies, and to decide which stocks and bonds may be listed for trading.

No one else is allowed on the trading floor, to keep distractions at a minimum. For this reason (and tradition), women are not employed in any job where access to the floor is necessary. Even though one woman actually owns a seat on the New York Stock Exchange, she is not allowed on the trading floor.

Brokers on the American Stock Exchange floor.

3

The Stockholder

What must a stockholder consider when investing in the market? There are several things, of varying importance, in addition to the key factor — the type of stock purchased. There are two types of stock: common and preferred. *Common stock* is the usual way a corporation divides its ownership. Common stockholders are paid dividends, based on the company's earnings, after dividends are paid to holders of bonds and preferred stock. The holders of *preferred stock* are paid dividends, usually fixed in amount, before those paid to common stockholders.

Stocks represent part-ownership in a company. The holders of preferred stock receive preference over common stockholders in regard to dividends.

Let us assume that we are talking about common stock in a large industrial corporation listed on the Big Board. The most vital consideration to the investor is appreciation, or growth, of invested capital. Appreciation means an increase in the stock's value, which will occur if the corporation is successful.

By selling his stock at a higher price than it cost, an investor can realize a better rate of profit than if his funds were left in a bank to earn interest. To a large extent, common stock ownership protects the investor's worth during inflationary periods, since the corporation's assets also increase in worth. Stock ownership, then, gives the stockholder the right to participate in the stock's market performance.

It should be remembered that not all stocks go up, that not every firm is successful, and that periodic fluctuations affect every stock. The success of specific corporations depends on their industry, the competence of management, quality of product, advertising, adequate supplies of labor, and many other factors. Therefore, the amount which investors consider to be a fair price for any stock changes as its situation shifts.

The typical established corporation pays *dividends*, portions of net income, to stockholders. The amount depends on the company's earning power, and usually is paid quarterly. Shareholders receive a dividend for each share they hold. Some companies do not pay dividends in cash, but in extra shares of stock. A 5 percent stock dividend, for example, would give five new shares to the present holder of each 100 shares, or round lot. But if the company fails to earn any money, or management does not declare dividends, they are not paid.

A worker operates the machine that sorts dividend checks. Some companies pay dividends in the form of extra shares of stock rather than in cash.

Another aspect of stock ownership is that it allows the investor to participate in a venture he could not otherwise afford. No individual could afford to own a large airline, for example, but by buying shares in American, United, or TWA, he can become a partial owner of those coast-to-coast carriers. It should be stressed, however, that this ownership is largely symbolic. That is, an individual who owns 100 or even 1,000 shares cannot try to participate in the company's management, because this would disrupt normal procedures.

Similarly, although the stockholder has the right to vote on company business, he has little power even when attending annual meetings. His shares are a tiny proportion of the total shares outstanding, with a majority vote needed to adopt any new policies. The company directors usually control a majority of votes, so that individual stockholders find it impossible to effect any changes.

Most investors are uninterested in company operations, so long as these operations are successful and the stock increases in value. With such a wide variety of stock to choose from, investors usually sell stocks that do not meet their objectives.

Corporate Obligation to Stockholders

Corporate responsibility to stockholders includes the sending of quarterly and annual reports, notices of annual meetings, and a prospectus if any new stock is to be issued. The stockholder is usually given an opportunity to subscribe to new issues in proportion to his present shares, in order to prevent his proportion of ownership (however small) from being reduced.

In recent years, the Securities and Exchange Commission has ruled that the corporation has an additional responsibility to its shareholders. It may not withhold information that would affect the stock's price while using the information for its own benefit.

In a case decided by the U.S. Circuit Court of Appeals in 1968, the court found that the Texas Gulf Sulphur Company (and its executives and directors) bought company stock in the open market *before* announcing a rich mineral find in Canada. They were also found guilty of passing this "inside" information on to selected friends. The SEC argued, and the court agreed, that shareholders of the company who sold their stock before this information was released were deprived of their right to know of the new development — in this case, finding copper and silver deposits. In April 1969, the United States Supreme Court agreed with these findings.

There is little else that a corporation is actually required to do for its stockholders. If the company, or its officers, do not unfairly profit from their inside knowledge of operating results, they do not have to make public any information except periodic summaries of profit or loss unless so requested by the SEC.

This is still a great improvement over 100 years ago, when a leading railroad responded to a request from the New York Stock Exchange for information by saying that it "made no reports, and published no statements, and has not done anything of the kind for the last five years." The exchange had to suspend the railroad's stock from trading until a report was eventually issued.

Should the corporation dissolve and go out of business, stockholders are entitled to a share of the assets, if any remain after bondholders and preferred stockholders are paid. If the firm fails, however, it is unlikely that any assets will remain for the common stockholders to share.

4

Securities Regulation
and the Public Interest

Although the rights of investors are better pro-
tected now, the history of securities trading indicates
that this has not always been so. Passage of state and
federal laws regulating brokers, stock exchanges, and
companies issuing stock, would not have occurred if
the need for reform had not existed.

Blue-Sky Laws

Until 1933, there was no federal regulation of the
securities industry. The first state law regulating securities was passed in Kansas in 1911. At that time, a

state legislator commented that unscrupulous promoters, if allowed, would try to sell shares in "the blue sky itself." Since then, all state statutes regulating securities are called *blue-sky laws*. While laws vary in each state, most of them now require registration of all brokerage firms and over-the-counter dealers, new issues of stock, and all bonds sold across state lines. Nevada is the only state without a blue-sky law.

The Securities and Exchange Commission

After the stock market crash of 1929, and during the depression that followed, Franklin D. Roosevelt ran for President. One of his pledges in the 1932 campaign was to regulate the stock market and its practices. Thousands of small investors who had lost all their money in the crash supported the idea and helped elect Roosevelt to office.

During President Roosevelt's first term, congressional hearings disclosed that prominent industrial and political figures had been involved in stock manipulation. Soon after these hearings, the Securities Act of 1933 was passed, requiring all issuers of corporate securities to register stocks sold through the mail or in interstate commerce, and to disclose information needed by investors. (Use of the mails and interstate commerce are both subject to federal rather than state control.)

This law was followed by the Securities Exchange Act of 1934, which set up the Securities and Exchange

Crowds fill Wall Street after the stock market crash of October 29, 1929.

Commission (SEC) to prevent the recurrence of excessive speculation and manipulation. The SEC has wide power to force compliance with the law, including the suspension of stocks from trading. The Commission can even halt entire exchanges if necessary, but has never done so.

The idea that investment bankers and brokers should assume greater responsibility was expressed best by Louis D. Brandeis, a U.S. Supreme Court justice from 1916 until 1939. In his book, *Other People's Money*, published in 1914, Brandeis said that financiers had an obligation to be more honest in handling the money entrusted to them.

At first, there was considerable reluctance on Wall Street — especially at the New York Stock Exchange — to cooperate with the new agency. This unwillingness occurred despite President Roosevelt's selection of Joseph P. Kennedy as the SEC's first chairman. A wealthy investor and Wall Street figure, Kennedy also is remembered as the father of our 35th President.

During the half-century before reform began, the business done by floor traders and brokers at the New York Stock Exchange was marked by a disregard for the public. Finally, in 1937, the SEC forced a reorganization of the exchange's governing board in order to restore public confidence in the stock market. This confidence had been badly shaken by the Great Depression, and also by evidence that widespread dishonesty had occurred on the trading floor. In 1938, Richard Whitney, a famous financier and former New York Stock Exchange president (from 1930 to 1935), was convicted of fraud and grand larceny for over $8 million. He went to prison.

Over the years, the SEC has conducted several studies of stock market activities and issued reports of its findings. As a result, more complete and detailed rules were put into effect to discourage dishonesty. A series of speculative waves during the late 1950s and in 1961 led to a thorough investigation of the American Stock Exchange in 1962. As a result, its president was forced to resign and two specialists were permanently suspended.

The SEC has been called a "watchdog" on Wall Street. Several years ago it extended its attention to large brokerage firms, and their use of "inside" information. Merrill Lynch, Pierce, Fenner and Smith, the nation's largest brokerage firm, was fined and had to close one of its underwriting offices temporarily in December 1968, as punishment in a widely publicized case.

Merrill Lynch, due to its size, is both an underwriter of new stock issues and a brokerage house dealing with the public. The SEC charged that information obtained from the Douglas Aircraft Corporation in 1966, in connection with a proposed bond offering, was used to warn certain favored customers of a drop in Douglas's earnings that had not been publicly announced. At the same time, Merrill Lynch was recommending Douglas stock to small investors. The SEC found this to be "fraud or deceit" against the public.

Because of the Merrill Lynch case, corporations and brokers are more alert to problems of this type. Their disclosure of information affecting stocks now conforms to the SEC's guidelines.

The SEC also makes administrative rulings that affect the market's structure. In early 1972 a report called for consolidating the stock tape, to make possible the viewing of trading activity in all markets for a single stock. For example, an issue traded on the Big Board, the Midwest, and in the third market could be followed simultaneously. Brokers could select the best price for their client, wherever the stock is sold.

Ultimately, this could lead to one nationwide market for all stocks. Such a development is not likely overnight, but scientific advances in computer technology and information systems have laid the foundation for eventual consolidation along these lines.

Other Regulations

Most federal regulation is under the Securities Act of 1933 and Securities Exchange Act of 1934, as later amended. There is also one other safeguard which regulates the activities of persons other than brokers who advise the public on stock.

The Investment Advisors Act of 1940 calls for registration of individuals or firms that compile research and sell the findings to investors. Advisors must, for example, disclose their ownership of any security they suggest to the public. They are also liable for deliberate misstatements or fraudulent representation of a company or its securities.

The Investment Company Act of 1940 regulates investment companies, which are also called *mutual funds*. Many individual investors buy shares in these companies, which then pool the proceeds and invest in securities. The primary advantages of this system are that it provides professional management for investors lacking knowledge of market conditions, and a share in a diversified portfolio of stocks for a small amount of money. The financial impact of mutual funds — total assets of registered companies increased 10-fold in recent years to over $53 billion — is reason enough for their activity to be regulated. Investors who put their money in this type of venture face the same risks as one finds in the market — fluctuation in stock value and uncertainty of profit.

According to a 1966 SEC study, some mutual funds charge too much for their services, and their installment contractors put investors at an initial disadvantage. The SEC recommended a reform of investment company practices to Congress. Legislation toward that end is now pending.

5

Objectives of Investment

Let us consider in more detail why people invest in securities. So far, we have talked only about common stocks, where appreciation (profit) of invested capital is considered the most important objective. For a majority of stockholders, that is the case. Others, however, depending on their age, financial reserves, obligations to support family and current income, may choose preferred stock or bonds to achieve their goals. *Bonds* are a corporation's written promise to repay, with interest, borrowed money. The bondholder earns a fixed return on his investment in the form of interest

A United States Savings Bond, Series E.

payments. If a company is dissolved, bondholders — as the company's creditors — must be paid before either preferred or common stockholders.

Current income is necessary for some investors. This income consists of steady dividends paid quarterly, or bond interest paid semi-annually. Elderly persons, who possess capital but are no longer able to work, favor the stocks or bonds that provide the highest safe income. Electric utilities and gas pipeline companies are examples of corporations whose securities return a high yield and make steady payments to shareholders. This is largely due to the nature of their business, which is more stable than manufacturing or advertising.

Safety of principal (the amount invested) is vital to some investors with only moderate reserves. For these persons, government bonds are the safest investment, but they pay a somewhat lower rate of return than high-quality industrial bonds. Investors in these securities do not expect their value to fluctuate greatly, but at least the money remains available to them.

Persons seeking both a steady current return and safety usually buy *fixed-income securities*, for which the amount and frequency of payment (quarterly dividends) are predetermined. Investors willing to accept greater risks buy either common stocks or convertible securities, whose value is related to common stocks. (Convertible securities will be discussed in Chapter Seven.)

Investors with very high incomes also must be aware of tax considerations. Dividends, except for the first $100 received annually, are taxable as normal income. For persons whose incomes are taxed at high rates, the profit after taxes on fixed-income securities can be low. Sometimes, it can even be less than the rate of economic inflation! In that case, the real value of an investment is reduced rather than increased.

For these reasons, *tax-exempt bonds* are a favorite investment of wealthy persons. Interest on bonds issued by the various states, and by certain local governments within them, are tax free to residents of those states. Since many of these bonds are issued by municipal governments, they are also known as *municipal bonds*.

Most investors, however, buy common stocks first, as a means of increasing the investor's current worth, and second, to keep this real worth from declining due to inflation. The weakness of fixed-income securities (except convertible ones) is the erosion of principal value over time. In the past 10 years, for example, prices have gone up by more than one-fifth, reducing the value of money (principal) by that amount.

6

Types of Investors

Just as there are various investment objectives, there are different approaches to investing in the stock market. Each approach represents an attitude, or way of selecting the stocks and bonds that make up a person's list. Investors refer to their total list of holdings as a *portfolio*.

Many persons can be characterized as conservative investors, buying only stocks in companies that are industry leaders with long records of uninterrupted earnings. These stocks are called *blue chips*, an expression meaning highest quality. Investors consider companies like IBM, Standard Oil of New Jersey,

Eastman Kodak, and Sears Roebuck to be in that category. Another pattern noted among conservative investors is their infrequent number of transactions. They select stocks carefully, then tend to hold them for longer time periods.

Medium-risk investors are less cautious and are willing to exchange stocks more frequently. Businessmen with experience in financial matters and stock ownership often fall into this group. Medium-risk investors look for situations in which price fluctuation affords profit opportunity, and are less dividend conscious than holders of blue chips. Therefore, the companies selected by medium-risk investors are often large and well known, but more subject to economic uncertainty. When future prospects are less certain, stocks tend to sell at lower prices. If this uncertainty is temporary, or moderate in nature, the stock is sometimes referred to as a "businessman's risk."

At the other extreme are *speculators*, or persons more concerned with a stock's market performance than its investment worth. Some, but not all, speculators buy unknown and obscure stocks, hoping for wider market interest to increase their value. Others buy securities of companies where great economic uncertainty is present.

Speculators frequently buy and sell stocks within the same day, or in a relatively short time. Many are willing to sell at a loss if their judgment proves faulty

The Conservative Investor.

and quickly reinvest in other areas, while more conservative investors would probably hold a stock for recovery if its overall record has been good. Speculators usually can make or lose the most money in a given time period, although some end up (after accepting more risks) in a position comparable to that of more conservative investors.

The idea of risk is, of course, relative. It can be viewed as a continuum, running from lesser to greater. Many investors balance their portfolio with some stocks from each category while emphasizing one specific type.

The Medium-Risk Investor.

The Speculator.

Many, but not all, speculators buy stocks on *margin*. When an investor buys stock on margin, he pays only part of the stock's total cost, borrows the remainder from his broker, and pays the broker interest on the loan. This technique — employed by the experienced investor — allows the investor to control more securities than he could otherwise afford.

The percentage that can be borrowed by investors buying on margin is determined by the Federal Reserve Bank. Early in 1972 it was 45 percent: for each $1000 of stock purchased on margin, $550 had to be put up and $450 borrowed by the investor. The interest brokers charge for margin loans is based on money-market rates — the rate of interest currently charged by banks for large commercial borrowing. Speculators must gamble on a stock's appreciating enough to absorb this additional cost.

The speculator watches fluctuating stock prices in order to predict whether prices will rise steadily into what is called a *bull market*, or will decline into a *bear market*. On Wall Street, a *bull* is someone who expects the market to rise, while a *bear* expects it to fall.

Speculators are sensitive to rumors, tips, and anything else that could influence their holdings. Sudden sharp price changes and unusually heavy trading volume are usually indicative of the presence of speculators in the market for a given stock.

7

Convertible Securities, Rights, Warrants, and Options

Convertible Stocks and Bonds

Thus far, we have emphasized common stocks in our discussion. However, other types of securities, known as *convertible securities*, are also traded. Both convertible bonds and preferred stock may be converted, or exchanged for common shares, at the holder's option. The *conversion ratio*, or number of common shares that can be obtained through this exchange, is fixed when the securities are first issued.

The conversion feature was first introduced to make bonds or preferred stock more attractive to potential investors. Corporations needing capital (the proceeds of a new securities issue) offered this privilege as an inducement to investors. Most new industrial bonds and many preferred stocks are now convertible.

Bonds and preferred stocks trade on the same exchange as the corporation's common stock, and are influenced by its price. For example, if a preferred stock can be converted into two shares of common stock, it would sell at nearly double the price. Fluctuations in the common stock's price are reflected in changes in the preferred stock. Stockholders owning the preferred stock are entitled to dividends declared by the directors before any dividends are paid on the common shares. Sometimes companies do not earn enough to pay common stock dividends, but they still must pay dividends on the preferred stock.

Convertible bonds operate in essentially the same way, except that by conversion the holder gives up his status as a creditor of the company and becomes a shareholder. Creditors have certain legal rights, including court action against the corporation for nonpayment of interest. Common stockholders, on the other hand, do not receive a dividend unless the corporate directors declare one.

Bonds are traded in $1,000 denominations, and can be converted into a specified number of shares. If the number of shares is 25, each share is worth $40 ($1,000÷25). After trading of the bond begins, its price varies according to the price of common stock. If the common stock goes up to $42, the bond's worth will climb to about $1,050 ($42×25). Because of the conversion privilege, bonds of this type are worth more to investors and sometimes sell at a higher price, or premium, over their conversion value.

Non-convertible bonds, on the other hand, sell at a price based on the economic cost of money (reflected in interest rates) and on the number of years until maturity. Another consideration applicable to all bonds is their quality as an investment. Less established, unstable companies must offer a higher rate of return on their bonds in order to offset their greater risk.

A corporation may call its bonds for redemption, at a predetermined price, prior to their maturity date. This is another reason that investors prefer convertible bonds. If the issue is called, its value does not suddenly drop to the call price but continues to reflect common stock prices until the last days before redemption. Bondholders have time to either convert to common stock or to sell the bonds at prices based on conditions under which they were bought.

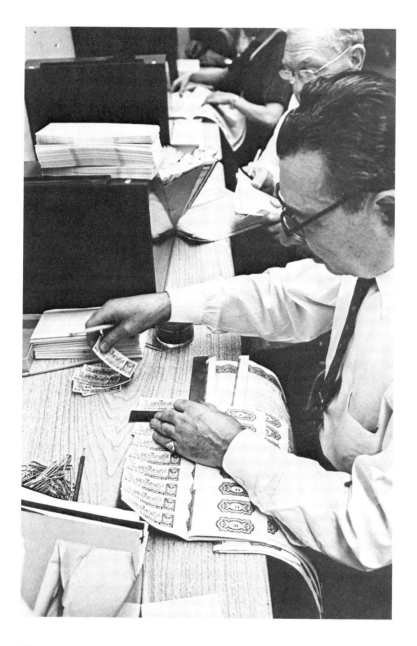

Rights

Because of interest rates or bond market conditions — or for other reasons — some firms try to raise money by issuing more common stock rather than by selling bonds or using other means of capitalization. When corporations issue additional common shares, they usually offer present stockholders the opportunity to retain a proportional share of stock ownership before the stock is offered to the public. A corporation increasing its capitalization by 25 percent, for example, must offer one share to holders of each existing four shares, by issuing them the right to subscribe at a discount in price. The offer to stockholders to buy some of the additional shares is known as the issue of *rights*.

The stockholder, on the other hand, may not want to increase his position in that stock. During a prescribed period, he can sell the rights to others, as they are traded wherever the common stock is listed.

Warrants

Another form of option is the *warrant*. Its holder is entitled to purchase a given number of common shares at a stated price for a certain stated period of time. Warrants are usually issued with preferred stock, but sometimes also with bonds. Corporations hope to attract investors to their securities by providing the "bonus" or extra inducement of warrants. Corporations use this tactic at times when market conditions may otherwise prevent the immediate sale of new securities.

Some warrants expire on given dates, others are perpetual or permanent until exercised. The *exercise price*, or sum to be paid by the holder in order to acquire the stock, is also stated by the corporation. This amount can be fixed for the warrant's life, or can change according to a schedule. It is not uncommon for a company whose securities trade on the New York Exchange to list its warrants on the American, as only stocks and bonds are permitted on the Big Board. Trans World Airlines (TWA), Gulf and Western Industries, Hilton Hotels, and the Atlas Corporation, among others, are examples of such companies.

Each TWA warrant, plus $22, entitles the holder to a share of common stock. The warrants expire December 1, 1973. In the meantime, investors can hold a claim on TWA's future prospects without buying its stock, through separate purchase of the warrants.

This privilege is also worth money. Early in 1972 TWA common stock sold for $56 a share. The warrants traded at about $38. Purchase of the TWA warrant plus the exercise price ($38 + $22 = $70) would be more expensive than buying TWA common stock ($56) directly. The difference ($70 − $56 = $14) is considered the warrant's premium.

Options

Contracts are available, at a fee, by which investors can arrange to buy or sell stocks at a predetermined price until a given date. A group of brokers specialize in writing these *options*, since trading of this nature is not permitted on exchange floors.

The use of options is otherwise quite legal, and in fact, it is a widespread practice on the part of investors willing to pay for the guarantee. The option to buy 100 shares of a particular stock is known as a *call*, while its opposite, a contract to sell 100 shares, is a *put*.

Puts and calls are written for an agreed time period, usually one, two, three, or six months. They are most frequently used by speculators either to profit on a small capital investment, or to prevent a gain from becoming a loss.

In the first instance, an investor buys a call on a stock he expects to go up. Consider this hypothetical case. With the price of General Motors at $80 per share, an investor buys a six-month call for $500. This sum entitles him to buy 100 shares of GM stock during the next six months for $80 a share. If the stock goes up to $95, for example, the profit on 100 shares would be almost double the investment. This is figured as $9,500 − $8,000 = $1,500 gross profit, less the option's (call's) cost ($1,500 − $500 = $1,000). After deducting the commission on the trades and taxes, the investor has about $900 profit remaining.

Workers on a General Motors assembly line. If an investor bought a put or a call on General Motors stock and the stock decreased in value, the investor would lose no more than the cost of the option.

The advantage of using a call is that $500 is the total amount the investor could have lost. If GM declined rather than went up, the call would be allowed to expire unexercised. For an investor to buy the stock rather than to buy a call on it, however, he would have to put up $8,000, plus commissions (unless he could borrow 20 percent of that amount on margin). The same price increase (from $80 to $95 per share) in General Motors stock would produce a profit of $1,500 (less commissions), or a return of about $1,400 — somewhat less than 20 percent on the invested capital. The investor using a call, during the same time, earned 80 percent on his money.

A put (contract to sell) is useful when the investor believes declining prices may be imminent. If the same man bought General Motors at $80 a share, and saw it go up to $95, he could buy a put if he did not want to sell the stock. One reason for his reluctance to sell might be taxes. The investor bought his GM stock only two and a half months ago, and gains on stocks held longer than six months are taxed at lower rates.

For about $350, the investor obtains a 90-day put. This allows him to sell 100 shares of General Motors, at $95 a share, any time during the next three months. If the stock goes down, his profit (less the cost of the put) is preserved, and can then be taken at the lower tax rate. If the stock goes up further, the put's cost is deducted from final profits, and can be considered insurance on a favorable outcome.

There are other forms of option contracts too complicated to discuss here. Some of them have interesting names, however, such as *straddles*, *strips*, and *straps*. These options are used mostly by sophisticated traders and speculators, not by the average investor.

8

Reading the Financial Pages

Most investors follow reports of trading in the daily press, except in areas where the local newspapers do not have sufficient coverage of business news. Many stockholders also read the *Wall Street Journal*, a daily paper devoted mainly to business news and stock market reports. The *Wall Street Journal* carries complete transaction reports from both the New York and American stock exchanges. How do we interpret the reports? The following illustration represents an actual summary for a day in 1969.

—1968-69—		Stocks Div.		Sales in 100s	Open	High	Low	Close	Net Chg.
High	Low								
66⅛	43½	Pittston	1.20b	105	58⅞	59	57¾	58	− ⅞
78½	56¾	Plough	.60	64	70	70	69½	69½	− ⅜
133⅝	**88**	**Polaroid**	**.32**	**735**	**118⅛**	**124½**	**117¾**	**122¾**	**+4¾**
28½	22⅛	Portec	1.20	13	26¾	27	26⅝	26¾	
85	77½	Porter	pf5.50	z100	84	84⅜	84	84⅜	+ ⅜

From The Wall Street Journal, *edition of Friday, January 10, 1969: a section from the list of New York Stock Exchange transactions for Thursday, January 9, 1969.*

Each stock is listed by name (or abbreviation) in alphabetical order. Take Polaroid stock as an example. To the left of the company's name are two numbers. These represent the highest and the lowest price at which Polaroid's stock traded during the preceding year (1968) and the first part of the current year (1969) up to the preceding day. By March, the quotations from the preceding year are dropped, and only the figures for the current year are given.

These numbers are followed by the name, Polaroid. (It is assumed that the company's investors will know that Polaroid is a manufacturer of cameras and other photographic equipment.) The next figure, .32, indicates an annual dividend rate of 32 cents per share. It is paid quarterly, at eight cents per share.

The column marked "sales" records trading volume. On this particular day, 735 round lots, or 73,500 shares, were traded. "Open" indicates the price of the morning's first trade — 118⅛. For 100 shares, that would be $11,812.50. The "high" or top price of the day was 124½, the "low" was 117¾, and the "last" or final trade before the close of trading was 122¾. The "net change," or difference from the previous day's closing price, was up 4¾, or $4.75 per share.

The *Wall Street Journal* is published by Dow Jones and Company, which also puts out the *Dow-Jones Averages*, the most widely followed index of stock market activity. There are four Dow-Jones Averages: one for prices of 30 major industrial stocks; one for 20 leading railroad stocks; one for 15 representative utilities; and one for a combination of the 65 stocks. All of these stocks are listed on the New York Stock Exchange and most of them, particularly the industrials, are blue chips such as General Motors, Standard Oil of New Jersey, Du Pont, and American Telephone.

The Dow-Jones Averages are computed constantly and are officially announced to brokers at half-hour intervals during the trading day. At first, the Dow-Jones Averages were computed by adding the current prices of the stocks together and dividing the total by the number of stocks. Later, in order to compensate for stock splits and the issuing of additional stock by companies in the averages, Dow Jones began using a mathematical divisor which it felt reflected these changes.

Another widely followed average is the *500-stock index* published by Standard and Poor's Corporation, the nation's largest securities research company. The 500-stock index is made up of 425 industrials, 50 utilities, and 25 rails. Standard and Poor's index is considered to be more scientific than the Dow-Jones Averages. It is computed by multiplying the price of each stock by the number of shares outstanding, so that the larger and more influential companies exert their proper influence on the average. The 500-stock index is used by the Federal Reserve Board and the Department of Commerce, as well as by many government officials and economists.

Other than the fact that Standard and Poor's and Dow Jones use different methods of computing their averages, there is one great point of difference: the Dow-Jones Averages are always given in figures about 10 times greater than those published by Standard and Poor's. For example, if the Dow-Jones Industrials stand at 900, the 500-stock index might be 93. Standard and Poor's figures are actually much closer to the average price of stocks traded on the Big Board. In fact, for years the New York Stock Exchange has tried to persuade Dow Jones to divide its index by 10 — with no success.

In 1966, the New York Stock Exchange began publishing its own official index which included all 1,200 common stocks listed on the exchange. This index is computed continuously and is announced on the exchange ticker at half-hour intervals. In addition to this composite index, the Big Board also puts out four group indexes for industrials, transportation, utilities, and finance. Unlike the Dow-Jones Averages, the starting figure used by the exchange index is close to the $50 average price of all listed shares.

Although stock market averages are a popular means of following market activity, one thing must be remembered: they do not predict what will occur in the future; rather, they summarize what has happened in the past. Furthermore, the performance of any individual stock may be quite different from the popular averages, due to special circumstances related to the given company.

There are other publications which try to provide information for investors, as well as for the research departments of brokerage firms. Most of these journals expect their readers to have a basic knowledge of economics, accounting, taxation, and finance. Not all investors do, of course, but they must compete in the market against others who are experienced in evaluating business conditions and stock price fluctuations.

9

The Growing Influence of
Institutional Investors

Although more Americans invest in corporate securities now than at any previous time, a growing percentage of trading is attributed to organizations, or *institutional investors*, rather than to individuals. Banks, insurance companies, private and government pension funds, and the investment companies, or mutual funds, mentioned earlier, are all institutional investors. What these organizations have in common is that the money they invest is entrusted to them by others.

Banks that invest in securities are known as institutional investors. Other institutional investors include insurance companies, private and government pension funds, and investment companies.

At the beginning of 1972, institutional investors were responsible for more than one-third of all trading on the New York Exchange. What effect does such a strong institutional influence have on the market?

Mutual funds have become important because, as a group, they have vast sums to invest and have become more aggressive. Until the mid-1960s, most mutual funds were conservative in their investment policies. Since then, many new funds have been heavy speculators, causing wild fluctuations and erratic markets in some stocks.

The SEC and others have studied the activities of institutional investors, particularly in the light of market conditions during the 1969-1970 recession. Preliminary research suggests that some short-term impact on prices has resulted, but no lasting or long-term differences have thus far been observed.

The studies are continuing, since the public interest and the protection of all investors may require additional rules covering large institutions in the market.

Conclusion

Investment in corporate securities is a fundamental part of our market economy. Few areas of our national life reflect the "American dream" like owning stocks and bonds. In fact, more than one out of every seven Americans, or 31.9 million people, were stockholders in mid-1972.

All persons under 21 are not permitted by law to own securities directly. But by becoming acquainted with the market, young people develop an advantage over those whose introduction is delayed.

Brokers on the New York Stock Exchange floor.

This book is not intended as a complete or total summary for the novice investor. It is simply a guide to understanding something about the market, written with the idea that almost everyone can benefit from the knowledge of how the stock market works.

Glossary

bear — An investor who expects stock prices to decline.

bear market — A period of falling stock prices, expressed by a drop in popular market averages.

bid — The amount a dealer will pay for a stock at a given time.

blue chips — Stocks of companies which are leaders in their industry and whose products or services are known to be of highest quality.

blue-sky laws — The name given to state laws regulating the sale of securities and other related activity.

Board of Governors — The officials of the New York Stock Exchange. They oversee all trading and enforce the exchange rules.

bond — A written promise to repay, with interest, borrowed money. Both corporate and government bonds are traded in the market.

bull — An investor who expects stock prices to rise.

bull market — A period of rising stock prices, expressed by an increase in popular market averages.

call — An option to buy stock at a predetermined price until a given date.

commission brokers — Brokers who represent member firms on the stock exchange floor for the purpose of trading securities. Also called floor brokers.

common stock — The usual method by which a corporation divides its ownership. Common stockholders receive dividends, depending on the company's earnings, after payments to bondholders and preferred stockholders are made.

conversion ratio — The number of common shares that can obtained by exchanging a convertible security.

convertible securities — The bonds or preferred stocks which can be exchanged for common stock at the holder's option.

dividends — Cash payments made by corporations to their shareholders, usually four times a year.

Dow-Jones Averages — An index of stock market activity.

exercise price — The amount that an investor must pay in cash, in addition to a warrant, in order to purchase common stock through the exercise of the warrant.

fixed-income securities — Stocks or bonds on which the amount and frequency of payment to holders are predetermined.

floor brokers — Brokers who trade securities on the exchange floor for member firms. Also called commission brokers.

institutional investors — Organizations which use the money entrusted to them by others to invest in securities.

make a market — The willingness of brokers and dealers to buy or sell certain securities.

margin — The investment technique of purchasing securities partly on credit. The investor borrows a portion of the amount due from his broker.

municipal bonds — Debt obligations of government units other than the federal government. Municipal bond interest paid to investors is usually exempt from federal income tax and from state tax in the states in which they are issued.

mutual funds — Investment companies that use the money entrusted to them to invest in securities for possible gain. Their capital is obtained by selling shares in the fund.

odd lots — Any number of shares less than the normal unit of trading.

odd-lot dealers — Special brokers who buy and sell stocks in odd lots.

offer — The price for which a dealer will sell stock at a given time.

offering — The initial public sale of securities by an underwriter.

options — Contracts that ensure investors the right to buy or sell stocks at a set price during a given time period.

orderly market — A market in which prices are neither erratic nor fluctuate in a wild or uncontrollable manner.

over-the-counter market — A network of brokers and dealers, connected by telephone and teletype, who trade stocks not listed on exchanges.

pink sheets — Quotations of prices for over-the-counter securities published daily on pink paper by the National Daily Quotation Service.

portfolio — The total list of securities held by an investor.

posts — Booths on the floor of stock exchanges where trading actually takes place.

preferred stock — A form of corporate capitalization which pays dividends, usually fixed in amount, to preferred shareholders.

prospectus — A booklet of information on a company issuing securities to the public. The publication of this information is required by law.

put — An option to sell stock at a predetermined price until a given date.

registered traders — Independent persons holding seats on stock exchanges who trade for their own account rather than representing or handling orders for others.

rights — The offer to stockholders to purchase additional shares of a company's stock in proportion to their existing holdings. This offer is made prior to the sale of these securities to the public.

round lot — The normal number of shares, usually 100, traded in each transaction.

seat — A membership in a stock exchange. A seat permits its holder to trade securities directly without paying commissions to others.

specialists — Brokers who also act as dealers of certain listed stocks. Specialists try to maintain an orderly market in their stocks by buying or selling from their own account.

speculators — Individuals who follow short-term market activity and trade in stocks where the risk and uncertainty are greatest. Speculators are mainly concerned with rapid price fluctuations.

Standard & Poor's stock index — An index of stock market activity. Used by government economists to measure average price levels in securities markets.

straddle — A special form of option contract used by sophisticated investors. It combines features of both puts and calls.

syndicate — A group of investment bankers who underwrite new securities issues which have a value too great for one underwriter to handle.

tax-exempt bonds — See municipal bonds.

third market — A form of trading in which listed stocks are sold over-the-counter.

two-dollar brokers — Independent registered traders who handle trades for busy floor brokers. Two-dollar brokers are paid a commission which at one time was two dollars per transaction.

underwriter — An investment banking firm that purchases new securities from a corporation for resale to brokers representing individual investors.

warrant — An option permitting investors to purchase a given number of common shares at a stated price during a certain stated period of time.

Index

the author . . .

Marc Rosenblum is assistant professor of economics at John Jay College, City University of New York. Before coming to John Jay he was on the research staff of the Industrial Relations Center, University of Minnesota. Rosenblum also has been an instructor at Hunter College, City University of New York, a private economic consultant and security analyst, and a freelance writer.

Mr. Rosenblum holds an M.A. degree from City University of New York and a Ph.D. from the University of Minnesota. His book reviews and essays have appeared in the *Financial Analysts Journal*, the *Congress Bi-Weekly*, and other publications.

When not engaged in academic and economic pursuits, Mr. Rosenblum enjoys skiing and photography.

OTHER BOOKS ON SOCIALLY
SIGNIFICANT TOPICS YOU MAY WISH TO READ

the real world of pollution

The WATERS of the Earth
The AIR We Breathe
The LAND We Live On
The Dangerous ATOM
The NOISE We Hear
The FOOD We Eat
The BALANCE of NATURE
The POPULATION Explosion

the real world of economics

American Economic History
Underdeveloped Countries
Economics of the Consumer
International Trade
The Labor Movement in the United States
The Law and Economics
Modern Trade Unionism
Money and Banking
How A Market Economy Works
The Stock Market
Taxes

the real life books

Horace Mann
How Men Discovered the World
Hunters of the Black Swamp
The Proudest Horse on the Prairie
Will Rogers

the In America books

The AMERICAN INDIAN in America
The CHINESE in America
The CZECHS & SLOVAKS in America
The DUTCH in America
The EAST INDIANS & PAKISTANIS in America
The ENGLISH in America
The FRENCH in America
The GERMANS in America
The GREEKS in America
The HUNGARIANS in America
The IRISH in America
The ITALIANS in America
The JAPANESE in America
The JEWS in America
The MEXICANS in America
The NEGRO in America
The NORWEGIANS in America
The PUERTO RICANS in America
The POLES in America
The RUSSIANS in America
The SCOTS & SCOTCH-IRISH in America
The SWEDES in America
The UKRAINIANS in America
The FREEDOM of THE PRESS in America
The FREEDOM of RELIGION in America
The FREEDOM of SPEECH in America

the real world - crisis and conflict

Color and People
People in Bondage
Protest, vol. I
Protest, vol. II

We specialize in publishing quality books for
young people. For a complete list please write:

Lerner Publications Company
241 First Avenue North, Minneapolis, Minnesota 55401